s **ago** our fathers brough... ...on
...ceived in **liberty** and dedicated
**created equal.** Now we are en-
whether that nation or any **nation**
...ng endure. We are met on a great
...to **dedicate** a portion of that field
...ho **here gave their lives** that
...r fitting and proper that we should
...not dedicate, we cannot consecrate,
...**rave men,** living and dead who
...far above our poor power to add or
...long remember what we say here,
...id here. It is for **us the living** rather
...ed **work** which they who fought
...ced. It is rather for us to be here
...before us—that from **these hon-**
...otion to **that cause** for which
...otion—that we here highly resolve
...**died in vain,** that **this nation**
...n of **freedom,** and that **govern-**
...le, **for the people** shall **not**

**—LINCOLN'S GETTYSBURG ADDRESS**

MAIRA
KALMAN

# Looking at
# LINCOLN

Nancy Paulsen Books ✺ An Imprint of Penguin Group (USA) Inc.

ONE DAY,
WHILE WALKING THROUGH THE PARK
ON MY WAY TO BREAKFAST
I SAW A VERY TALL MAN.
HE REMINDED ME OF SOMEONE,
BUT I COULD NOT THINK WHO.

AT THE COFFEE SHOP I ORDERED PANCAKES.
THEY WERE DELICIOUS.

WE PAID WITH A LINCOLN

And TWO WASHINGTONS.

And THEN I REMEMBERED.
THE MAN I had SEEN LOOKED EXACTLY
LIKE ABRAHAM Lincoln.

**Abraham Lincoln.**

**The sixteenth president of the United States.**

WHO WAS HE? I WENT TO THE LIBRARY TO FIND OUT.
ABRAHAM Lincoln WAS such AN AMAZING MAN THAT
THERE ARE OVER 16,000 Books WRITTEN ABOUT him.
I WANTED TO READ Them ALL, BUT I GOT LOST IN
PHOTOS OF his UNUSUAL FACE.
I STARED AT ONE.
I COULD Look AT him FOREVER.

He was born in a small log cabin
in Kentucky on February 12, 1809.
The family was poor.
Abe was a dreamer. He did not like to do chores.
He loved to read.

HE WAS LUCKY. HIS STEPMOTHER LOVED him LIKE CRAZY.
AND HE ADORED HER.

SHE LOOKS SO STERN, BUT SHE LET him DREAM
AND READ AS MUCH AS HE WANTED.

*Subtraction of Long Mea...*

| £ | M | f | P |
|---|---|---|---|
| 7 | 1 | 3 | 10 |
| 44 | 2 | 5 | 16 |
| 21 | 1 | 5 | 34 |
| 11 | 1 | 3 | 50 |

*Subr*

| Y | l | T | B |
|---|---|---|---|
| 48 | 0 | 1 | 2 |
| 12 | 0 | 3 | 1 |
| 36 | 0 | 10 | 1 |
| 48 | 0 | 1 | 2 |

## Of Land Measure

| A | R | P |
|---|---|---|
| | 4 | 40 |
| 12 | 1 | 10 |
| 5 | 3 | 17 |
| 6 | 1 | 33 |
| 12 | 1 | 10 |

| A | R | P |
|---|---|---|
| | 4 | 40 |
| 17 | 3 | 17 |
| 12 | 3 | 23 |
| 4 | 3 | 34 |
| 17 | 3 | 17 |

| a | R | P |
|---|---|---|
| | 4 | 40 |
| 28 | 1 | 7 |
| 19 | 1 | 28 |
| 8 | 3 | 19 |
| 28 | 1 | 7 |

## Of Dry Measure

| Ch | B | P |
|---|---|---|
| | 36 | 4 |
| 17 | 2 | 1 |
| 10 | 9 | 3 |
| 7 | 0 | 2 |
| 17 | 2 | 1 |

| Ch | B | P |
|---|---|---|
| | 36 | 4 |
| 50 | 1 | 2 |
| 16 | 5 | 1 |
| 23 | 32 | 1 |
| 30 | 7 | 2 |

| Ch | B | P |
|---|---|---|
| | 8 | 4 |
| 19 | 1 | 1 |
| 12 | 7 | 2 |
| 6 | 1 | 3 |
| 19 | 1 | 1 |

Abraham Lincoln
his hand and pen
he will be good but
god knows when

He went to school for only one year.

But he was curious and taught himself many things.

THEY had HARdLY ANY SUPPLIES.

And of course, no electricity.
Abraham spent many hours
reading by the fire's glow.

One day he was kicked in the head by a mule.
He slept for two days.
Then he woke up and grew up
and decided to be a lawyer.

(HE did LiKE TO ARGUE.)

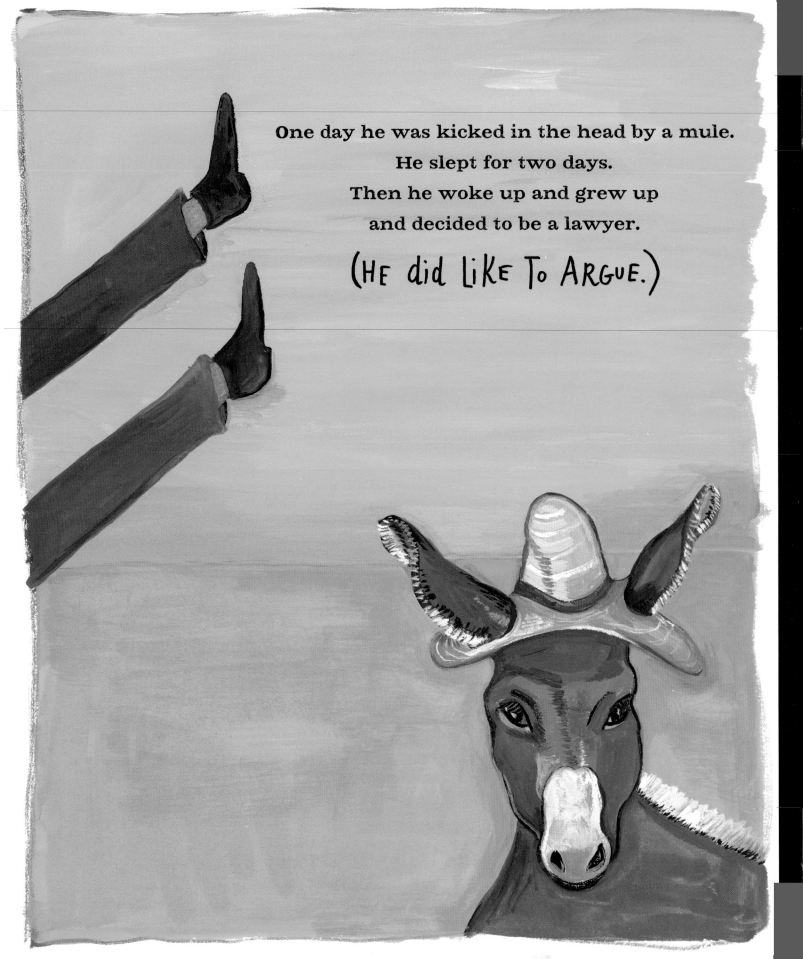

He lived in Springfield, Illinois.
And got a reputation as a smart and honest man.
They called him Honest Abe.

He had a family that he loved very much.
His wife, Mary (who was very short), and four sons.
They laughed and had lots of friends and
even ran around a little wild.

I WONDER IF MARY And ABRAHAM
HAd NICKNAMES FOR EACH OTHER.
DiD SHE CALL Him LiNKY?
DiD HE CALL HER LiTTle PLUMPY?
MAYBE.

Abe worked hard and
became interested in the government.
He decided he would run for president.
And on March 4, 1861,
he was inaugurated
president of the United States.

ON the DAY HE WAS ELECTED
I BET MARY MADE his FAVORITE VANILLA CAKE.

BUT MAYBE he FORGOT TO EAT his SLICE.
HE WAS OFTEN TOO BUSY Thinking to EAT.

Lincoln wore a very tall hat.

(With his hat on he was seven feet tall.)

He wrote many notes and stuffed them inside his hat.

WHAT WAS hE THINKING ABOUT?

He was thinking about democracy.
The Declaration of Independence and the Constitution
created by the founders of this country.

He was thinking
about freedom and
doing good for mankind.

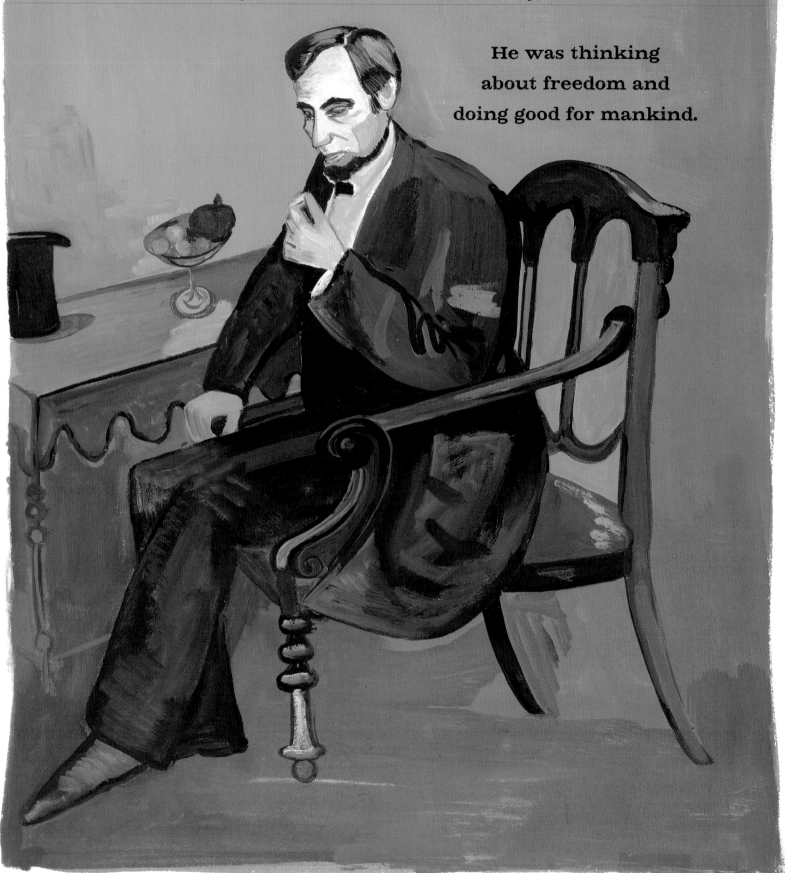

And MAYBE HE WAS ALSO THINKING ABOUT
GETTING A BIRTHDAY PRESENT for his
LITTLE SON.

MAYBE A WHISTLE.

OR PICK UP STICKS.

# WHAT did he LOVE?

He loved his dog Fido.

I THINK FIDO WAS CROSS-EYED.

He loved apples.
Cox's orange pippins.
White pippins.
Winesap.
Benoni.

He always had an apple on his desk.

He loved music. He loved Mozart.

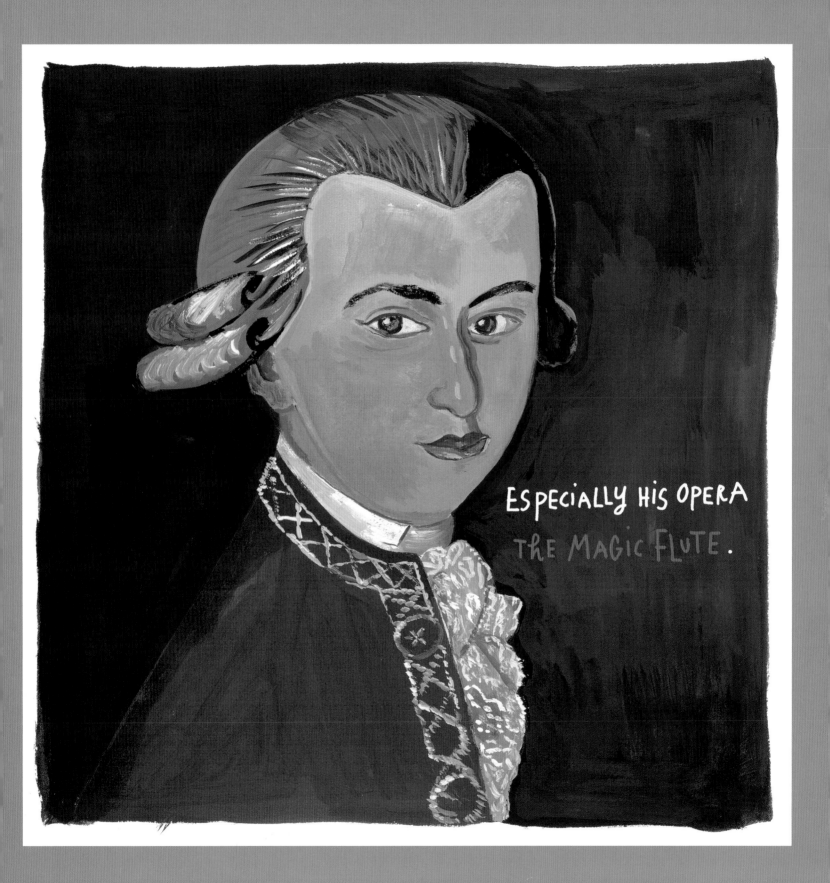

ESPECIALLY HIS OPERA
THE MAGIC FLUTE.

But mostly he loved people. His family, of course,
but all people. And he wanted them to live well.
He loved justice and truth.

The country was in trouble
and headed for a war.
After hundreds of years of slavery,
people were saying ENough.

There were courageous people
who fought for liberty,
like Sojourner Truth.

And Frederick Douglass, who had been a slave
until he ran away to the North.

Both of them met with
Lincoln and spoke of
the plight of slaves.

Lincoln **hated** slavery and wrote to a friend,

**"If slavery is not wrong, nothing is wrong."**

During his presidency
he issued the Emancipation Proclamation,
the first official step
toward freeing millions of slaves.

It was a difficult time to be president.

The Southern states (the Confederacy) wanted

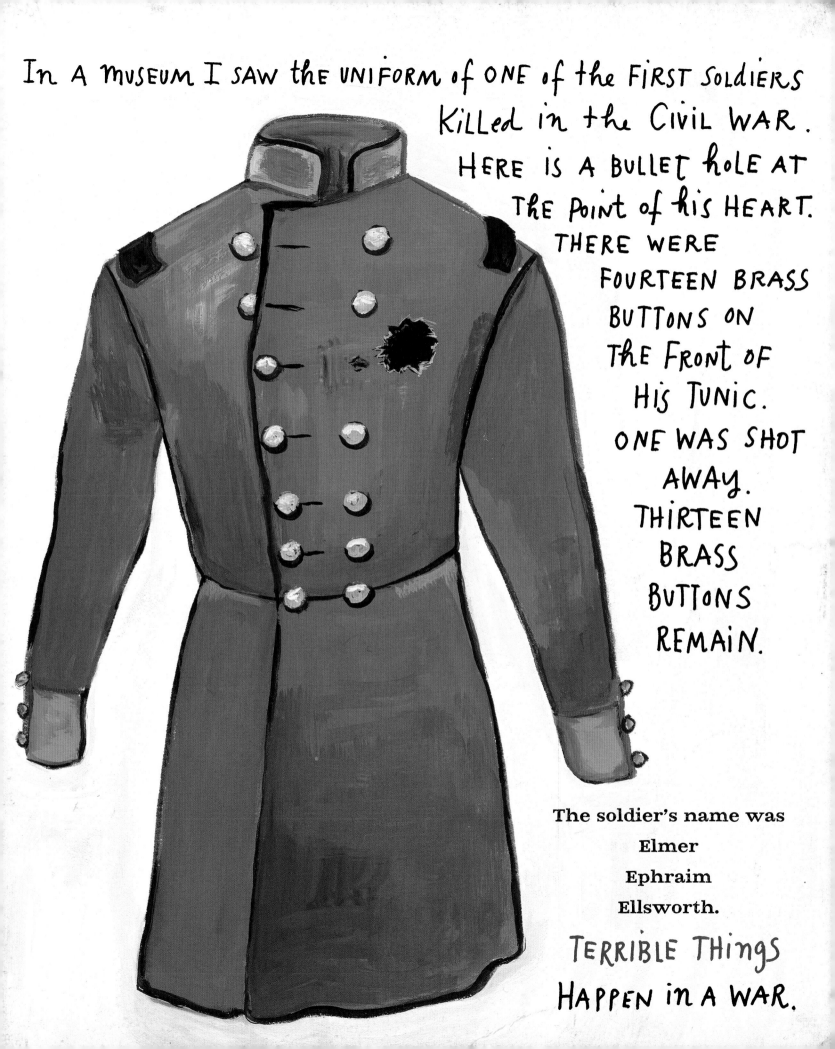

In A MUSEUM I SAW the UNIFORM of ONE of the FIRST SOLDiERS KiLLed in the CiViL WAR. HERE iS A BULLET hOLE AT the Point of hiS HEART. THERE WERE FOURTEEN BRASS BUTTONS ON THE FRONT OF HiS TUNiC. ONE WAS SHOT AWAY. THiRTEEN BRASS BUTTONS REMAiN.

The soldier's name was Elmer Ephraim Ellsworth.

TERRiBLE THiNgs HAPPEN in A WAR.

The Civil War ground on.
Lincoln went to Gettysburg, Pennsylvania, the site of a big battle.
Thousands of soldiers were buried there.
Many with just a number on their grave.

On that sad land,
Lincoln gave one of history's greatest speeches,
the Gettysburg Address.
It was short—only 272 words—ending with

"... government of the people, by the people,
for the people
shall not perish from the earth."

The war finally ended in 1865. Almost a million people
had been killed or wounded. The North had won.

The people had suffered greatly,
but now it was time to rejoice
and start to rebuild the country
with Lincoln leading the way.

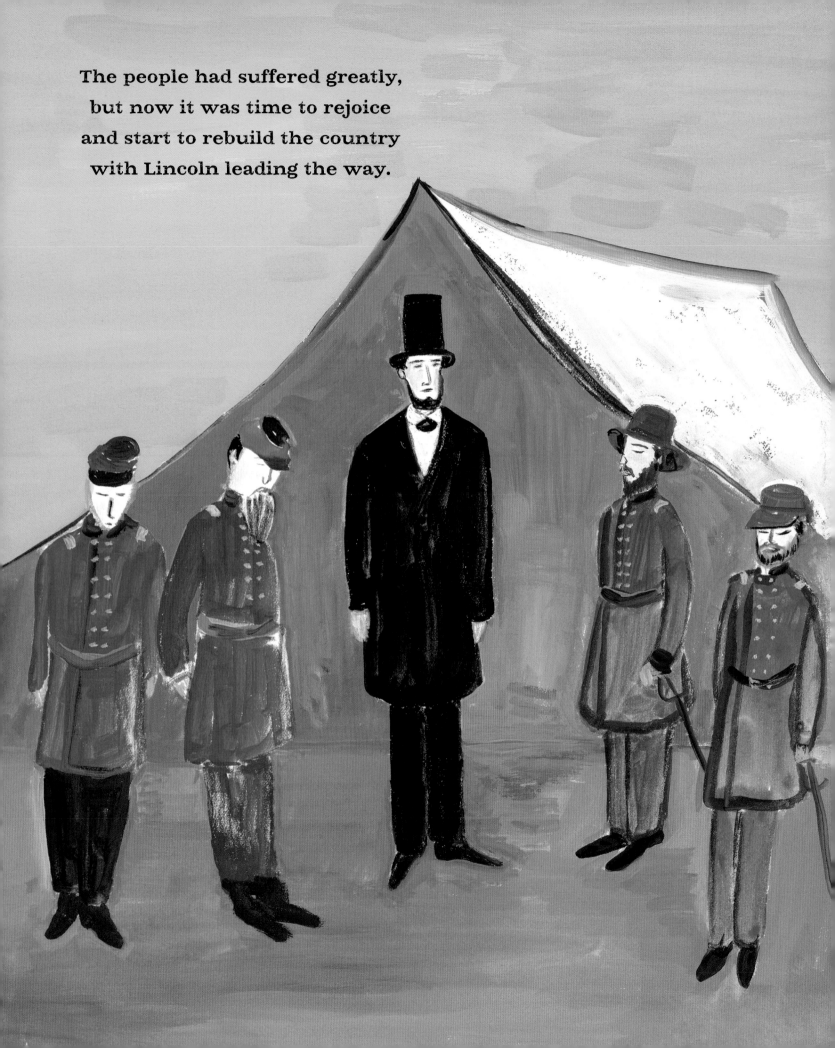

But it was not to be.

After the agony of the war,

Lincoln wanted to lighten the mood.

He took his wife to see a funny play.

During the play, he was shot.

MURDERED by A WRETCHED MAN
who DID NOT WANT SLAVERY TO END.

Lincoln had been rocking in this chair.
People carried him across the street
to the home of a friend.
He died the next morning, April 15, 1865.
He was fifty-six years old.

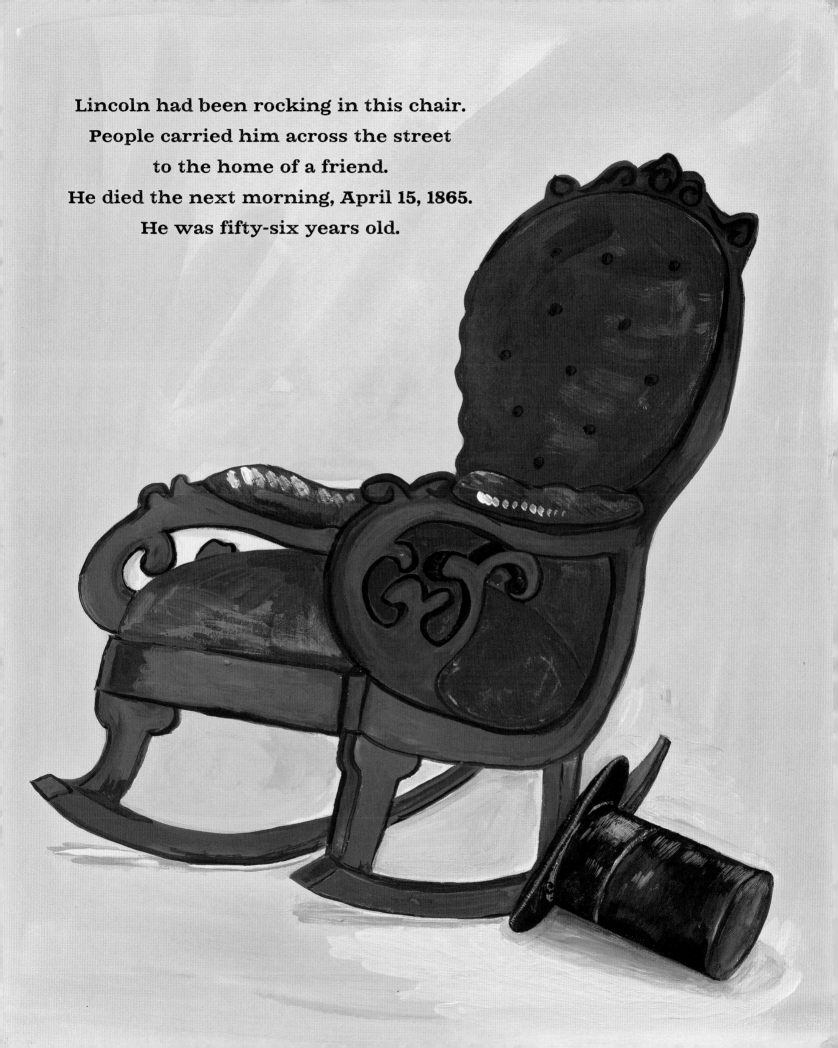

The news spread.
People across the land wept with
grief for their fallen leader.

ABRAHAM LINCOLN
WILL LIVE FOREVER.
And if you go to
WASHINGTON, D.C.
in the SPRING
you can WALK

Through the CHERRY BLOSSOMS And VISIT him.

AT his MEMORIAL YOU CAN READ THE WORDS HE WROTE NEAR THE END OF THE WAR.

"... With malice toward none, with charity for all."

And YOU CAN LOOK into his BEAUTIFUL EYES.
JUST LOOK.

# NOTES

**LINCOLN PRESENTERS:**
Impersonators of the sixteenth president visit schools, libraries and historical societies to bring Lincoln to life. The ideal impersonators are 6 foot 4 inches, just like Lincoln. There is even an Association of Lincoln Presenters, whose motto is "We are ready, willing and ABE L."

**LINCOLN'S LOG CABIN:**
Lincoln's family migrated west to Illinois, where they built their simple log cabin. The Illinois Historic Preservation Agency operates a site with a reproduction of the cabin.

**LINCOLN'S STEPMOTHER:**
Abraham Lincoln's mother, Nancy, died in 1818, when he was nine years old. A year later his father, Thomas Lincoln, married Sarah Bush Johnston, a widow with three children. She encouraged Abraham's love of reading, and he was very fond of her and always referred to her as "Mother."

**KICKED IN THE HEAD:**
In his tenth year, Lincoln was kicked in the head by a horse or a mule (there are varying accounts), and for a brief time he was thought to be dead.

**LINCOLN'S CHILDREN:**
Lincoln had four sons: Robert Todd, Edward Baker (Eddie), William Wallace (Willie), and Thomas (Tad). Eddie died as a toddler, and Willie died in the White House at age eleven.

**LINCOLN'S FAVORITE CAKE:**
Mary Todd first baked a vanilla-almond cake for Abraham Lincoln when they were courting. She made it when she was a Springfield housewife and when she was First Lady.

**LINCOLN'S DOG:**
Fido lived with the Lincoln family in Springfield, Illinois. The mixed-breed dog had to be left behind when the family moved to D.C., as he was terrified of loud noises and Lincoln feared the trip would be too much for him. Some neighbors happily took Fido and his favorite sofa in.

**SOJOURNER TRUTH:**
Sojourner Truth was a traveling preacher who fought for the abolition of slavery and for women's rights. Her most famous speech was called "Ain't I a Woman?"

**FREDERICK DOUGLASS:**
Douglass published his autobiography NARRATIVE OF THE LIFE OF FREDERICK DOUGLASS, AN AMERICAN SLAVE, WRITTEN BY HIMSELF to much acclaim and popularity. During the Civil War he fought for the rights of the African American Union Army.

**EMANCIPATION PROCLAMATION:**
President Abraham Lincoln issued the Emancipation Proclamation on January 1, 1863, during the Civil War. The proclamation declared that "all persons held as slaves" within the rebellious states "shall be then, thenceforward, and forever free."

**CIVIL WAR–ERA FLAG:**
The flag of the United States during the first half of the Civil War had 34 stars, one for every state of the Union, even those attempting secession. The 33rd star represented Oregon and the 34th Kansas.

**CIVIL WAR UNIFORMS:**
Early in the war, uniforms were supplied by individual towns and states, so there was a confusing variety. Over time, blue became the color for the North and gray for the Confederate South.

**COLONEL ELMER EPHRAIM ELLSWORTH:**
Ellsworth was a personal friend of Lincoln's and one of the Union's most promising officers. He was shot in Alexandria, Virginia, in May 1861, after removing a Confederate flag from atop a local inn. His sensational death was the first officer casualty on the front.

**GETTYSBURG ADDRESS:**
Lincoln's speech, delivered on November 19, 1863, at the Soldiers' National Cemetery in Gettysburg, Pennsylvania, is one of the most famous speeches in United States history.

**LINCOLN'S MURDER:**
Lincoln was watching a play called OUR AMERICAN COUSIN at Ford's Theatre in Washington, D.C., on April 14, 1865, when he was shot by John Wilkes Booth, actor and Confederate sympathizer. The gun used was a Philadelphia Deringer pistol, on display at the museum in Ford's Theatre.

The chair in which Lincoln was shot is on display at the Henry Ford Museum in Dearborn, Michigan.

**LINCOLN'S FUNERAL:**
Lincoln was buried in Springfield, Illinois, where he was honored with the military tradition of a riderless horse in his funeral procession. Lincoln's own horse, Old Bob, carried a pair of boots reversed in the stirrups to represent the fallen leader looking back on his troops for the last time.

**LINCOLN MEMORIAL:**
The nineteen-feet-tall marble statue of Lincoln was built under the supervision of sculptor Daniel Chester French. An inscription above the statue reads: "In this temple, as in the hearts of the people for whom he saved the Union, the memory of Abraham Lincoln is enshrined forever." Martin Luther King Jr. delivered his famous "I Have a Dream" speech from the steps of the Memorial.

# SOURCES

Holzer, Harold, ed. Abraham Lincoln: Portrayed in the
Collections of the Indiana Historical Society.
Indianapolis: Indiana Historical Society Press, 2006.

Jennison, Keith W. The Humorous Mr. Lincoln. New York:
Thomas Y. Crowell Co., 1965.

Junior League of Springfield, Illinois. Honest to Goodness:
Honestly Good Food From Mr. Lincoln's Hometown.
Nashville: Favorite Recipes Press, 2004.

Kunhardt, Philip B., III; Peter W. Kunhardt; and Peter W.
Kunhardt Jr. Looking for Lincoln: The Making of
an American Icon. New York: Alfred A. Knopf, 2008.

Lorant, Stefan. Lincoln: A Picture Story of His Life.
New York: Bonanza Books, 1979.

McCreary, Donna D. Lincoln's Table: A President's Culinary
Journey from Cabin to Cosmopolitan. Charlestown, Ind.:
Lincoln Presentations, 2008.

Mellon, James, ed. The Face of Lincoln. New York:
Viking Press, 1979.

Meredith, Roy. Mr. Lincoln's Camera Man: Mathew B. Brady.
New York: Charles Scribner's Sons, 1946.

Rubenstein, Harry R. Abraham Lincoln: An Extraordinary Life.
Washington, D.C.: Smithsonian Books, 2008.

Sandburg, Carl. Abraham Lincoln: The Prairie Years and
the War Years. New York: Harcourt, Brace and Co., 1954.

Schwartz, Thomas F. Mary Todd Lincoln: First Lady
of Controversy. Springfield, Ill.: Abraham Lincoln
Presidential Library Foundation, 2007.

Wills, Chuck. Lincoln: The Presidential Archives.
New York: DK Publishing, 2007.

Wilson, Douglas L. Honor's Voice: The Transformation
of Abraham Lincoln. New York: Alfred A. Knopf, 1998.

this one is for abe

and

for lulu and alex

**NANCY PAULSEN BOOKS**
A division of Penguin Young Readers Group.
Published by The Penguin Group.
Penguin Group (USA) Inc., 375 Hudson Street,
New York, NY 10014, U.S.A.
Penguin Group (Canada), 90 Eglinton Avenue East,
Suite 700, Toronto, Ontario M4P 2Y3, Canada
(a division of Pearson Penguin Canada Inc.).
Penguin Books Ltd, 80 Strand, London WC2R 0RL, England.
Penguin Ireland, 25 St. Stephen's Green, Dublin 2, Ireland
(a division of Penguin Books Ltd.).
Penguin Group (Australia), 250 Camberwell Road,
Camberwell, Victoria 3124, Australia
(a division of Pearson Australia Group Pty Ltd).
Penguin Books India Pvt Ltd, 11 Community Centre,
Panchsheel Park, New Delhi - 110 017, India.
Penguin Group (NZ), 67 Apollo Drive, Rosedale, Auckland 0632,
New Zealand (a division of Pearson New Zealand Ltd).
Penguin Books (South Africa) (Pty) Ltd, 24 Sturdee Avenue,
Rosebank, Johannesburg 2196, South Africa.
Penguin Books Ltd, Registered Offices: 80 Strand,
London WC2R 0RL, England.

Published simultaneously in Canada.
Manufactured in China by South China Printing Co. Ltd.

Design by Marikka Tamura.
Text set in Zapatista.
The art was done in gouache.
Library of Congress Cataloging-in-Publication Data
is available upon request.

ISBN 978-0-399-24039-3
1 3 5 7 9 10 8 6 4 2

Fourscore and seven yea

this continent a new nation,

to the proposition that all men a

gaged in a great civil war, testin

so conceived and so dedicated can

battlefield of that war. We have con

as a final resting-place for those

that nation might live. It is altogeth

do this. But in a larger sense, we ca

we cannot hallow this ground. The

struggled here have consecrated

detract. The world will little note n

but it can never forget what they

to be dedicated here to the unfinis

here have thus far so nobly adva

dedicated to the great task remaini

ored dead we take increased de

they gave the last full measure of d

that these dead shall not hav

under God shall have a new bir

ment of the people, by the peo

perish from the eart